Dear Aunt Staci:
I can't wait to meet you on December 13

Life's BIG Little Moments

AUNTS

Life's BIG Little Moments

AUNTS

SUSAN K. HOM

PHOTOGRAPHY BY JEFFREY H. MANTLER

STERLING

New York / London
www.sterlingpublishing.com

For my aunts, Linda, Emily, and Oy, with love

STERLING and the distinctive Sterling logo are registered trademarks of
Sterling Publishing Co., Inc.

Library of Congress Cataloging-in-Publication Data

Hom, Susan K.
   Life's big little moments : aunts / Susan K. Hom ; photography, Jeffrey H. Mantler.
       p. cm.
   ISBN 978-1-4027-5838-6
   1. Aunts--Anecdotes. 2. Aunts--Pictorial works. I. Mantler, Jeffrey H. II.
Title.
HQ759.94.H67 2008
306.87--dc22

                              2008013622

10 9 8 7 6 5 4 3 2 1

Published by Sterling Publishing Co., Inc.
387 Park Avenue South, New York, NY 10016
© 2008 by Sterling Publishing Co., Inc.
Distributed in Canada by Sterling Publishing
c/o Canadian Manda Group, 165 Dufferin Street
Toronto, Ontario, Canada M6K 3H6
Distributed in the United Kingdom by GMC Distribution Services
Castle Place, 166 High Street, Lewes, East Sussex, England BN7 1XU
Distributed in Australia by Capricorn Link (Australia) Pty. Ltd.
P.O. Box 704, Windsor, NSW 2756, Australia

Page 18 photo: Judee Herr
Page 21 photo: © PhotoCreate/shutterstock.com
Page 23 photo: Christine Bulger
Page 50 photo: © Tara Moore/Getty Images, Inc.
Page 59 photo: Kathryn Decaroli

Page 62 photo: © illusionstudio/shutterstock.com
Page 71 photo: Margaret LaSalle
Page 74 photo: Kim Sperandeo
Page 80 photo: Amy Conlon
Page 95 photo: Alison Horn

Sterling ISBN 978-1-4027-5838-6

For information about custom editions, special sales, premium
and corporate purchases, please contact Sterling Special Sales
Department at 800-805-5489 or specialsales@sterlingpublishing.com.

Introduction

Aunts are always up for adventure—whether it's a trip to the science museum or a marathon game of go-fish. Brimming with amusing family stories to tell, aunts help nieces and nephews discover new experiences and places. Aunts love joining in on all sorts of celebrations, including birthdays, school plays, and family gatherings.

Nieces and nephews remind aunts how much fun it is to be a kid. They introduce their aunts to their favorite books, thinking spots, and so, so much more—and sometimes aunts even engage in a little harmless mischief with their nieces and nephews.

All year round, aunts and their nieces and nephews share all kinds of moments—from a tear-inducing laugh at the movies to a warm hug at a wedding. In all of life's BIG little moments, aunts, nieces, and nephews appreciate one another and simply cherish their time together.

Nieces lead aunts

around the playground.

Aunts show nieces

that slides aren't just for kids.

Aunts tickle nephews

when they're acting shy.

Nephews tell aunts

about what they're learning in school.

Aunts tell nieces

how beautiful they are.

Nieces ask aunts

for their beauty secrets.

Nieces show aunts

that they can do a perfect cartwheel.

Aunts teach nieces

how to master the hula hoop.

Nephews help aunts
get to the next level in their favorite video game.
Aunts cheer nephews
on as they pass their high score.

Nieces beg aunts

to take them swimming on hot summer days.

Aunts remind nieces

to take a break every once in a while.

Nephews let aunts

enter their special fort—

if they know the secret password.

Aunts help nephews

defend the fort from invasion.

Nieces ask aunts

to help them study for a spelling test.

Aunts help nieces

sound out the complicated words.

Aunts remind nieces

that there is always time for a hug.

Nieces show aunts

that a hug can turn into a cuddle.

Nieces introduce aunts

to their new furry friends.

Aunts help nieces

come up with the perfect name.

Nephews ask aunts

about the animals they see at the zoo.

Aunts teach nephews

how to make different animal sounds.

Aunts tell nephews

funny stories about when they were young.

Nephews remind aunts

that youth is timeless.

Aunts show nieces

how to knit a scarf.

Nieces help aunts

stay hip to new trends.

Nephews show aunts

their shuffling skills.

Aunts teach nephews

the rules of the game.

Nephews

confide in aunts.

Aunts

assure nephews that their secrets are safe.

Nieces admire aunts

for their creativity.

Aunts encourage nieces

to pursue a hobby.

Nieces help aunts

celebrate the holidays.

Aunts always give nieces

the coolest presents—*never* socks.

Aunts tell nephews

how proud they are of them.

Nephews inspire aunts

to make the most of every day.

Aunts invite nieces

to share in their special day.

Nieces promise aunts

that they won't get their dress dirty.

Nieces urge aunts

to roll around in the grass

every once in a while.

Aunts encourage nieces

to be confident in who they are.

Nephews

play catch with aunts.

Aunts

show nephews how to catch the super-high ones.

Aunts take nieces

to see their favorite play.

Nieces remind aunts

that the theater is magical.

Nephews ask aunts

for a piggyback ride around the house.

Aunts tell nephews

to saddle up.

Nieces look to aunts

for help sometimes.

Aunts assure nieces

that they will always lend a hand.

Nephews can't wait

for aunts to come visit.

Aunts tell nephews

about all of the mischievous things

they did as kids.

Nieces

know how to cheer up aunts.

Aunts

pepper nieces with affectionate kisses.

Aunts make nieces

feel extra-special on their birthday.

Nieces inspire aunts

to ditch their diet and eat cake.

Nieces twirl for aunts

in their new dress.

Aunts whisper to nieces,

"You look just like a princess."

Nieces take aunts

for long walks in the park.

Aunts tell nieces

that autumn is their favorite season.

Aunts

enjoy catching up with nephews.

Nephews

reminisce with aunts about old times.

Aunts

recommend must-read books to their nieces.

Nieces

like discussing their favorite parts with aunts.

Nephews

enjoy their aunts' famous meatballs.

Aunts

show nephews how to twirl spaghetti
with a spoon.

Aunts introduce nephews

to family traditions.

Nephews help aunts

dye eggs for an Easter egg hunt.

Nephews

turn to aunts for advice.

Aunts

remind nephews that they'll always lend an ear.

Aunts

introduce nieces to fine jewelry.

Nieces

smile from ear to ear when aunts are visiting.

Aunts

arrive with surprise presents for nieces.

Nieces

beg aunts to bring them lip gloss.

Aunts

share inside jokes with nephews.

Nephews

make aunts laugh until they tear up.

Nieces remind aunts

of sweet little angels.

Aunts give nieces

gentle kisses on the cheek.

Nieces look to aunts

for fashion inspiration.

Aunts encourage nieces

to be true to themselves.

Nephews give aunts

a play-by-play of the big game.

Aunts resist reminding nephews

that they saw everything from the stands.

Aunts tell nieces

to follow their dreams.

Nieces remind aunts

to live life to the fullest.

Nephews look to aunts

for their wisdom.

Aunts remind nephews

to see things from different points of view.

Aunts show nieces

how to take care of a garden.

Nieces promise aunts

that they will water it every day.

Aunts show nieces

many tender moments.

Nieces make aunts

appreciate silent moments.

Nieces help aunts

reexperience the wonder of childhood.

Aunts encourage nieces

to wish big.